# Charles Deering Forecasts the Weather & Other Poems

Also by C.M. Clark:

*The Blue Hour*

*Pillow Talk* (with painter Georges LeBar)

# Charles Deering Forecasts the Weather & Other Poems

C.M. Clark

ISBN 978-1-105-61833-8

Illustrations and Design by Mari Pasita Andino

solutionholepress@gmail.com

Grateful acknowledgment is made to *Painted Bride Quarterly* where “Ismene Upstaged” is scheduled to appear. Some of the poems in Other Celebrities have appeared previously in *The Blue Hour*.

The poems in this collection are the product of my two years as Poet in Residence at the Deering Estate in Miami, Florida. Many thanks to Deering Estate staff for access to their photo archives and historical records.

*for Anne & Laura --*

*blue skies & sunny days*

*Charles Deering Forecasts the Weather* is a verse narrative that virtually reconstructs the life and landscape of early 20th Century industrialist Charles Deering who wintered in South Dade County, Florida, during the last years of his life.

This is a work of fiction. The historical facts and details of lived lives form the basis of these poems; the embellishments are imagined.

*Je est un autre.*

~ Rimbaud

# Contents

## Charles Deering Forecasts the Weather

## Other Celebrities

# Charles Deering
# Forecasts the Weather

# Charles Deering Forecasts the Weather

The Deering Estate lies a blunt half mile east
of my scant acres. What might be
their soup cook's quarters or

the Sunday kitchen. No, Deering doesn't really lie;
rather it sits, in some lights, squats, to hunker
on its limestone eggnest, sweet creek

spring water secretly running

running nearby. I like having
and knowing this great vestibuled folly --
windvane for snail's bone -- stands

between me and the bay. And out beyond
where the shameless ocean shifts back and forth.
Having Deering's legacy --

an older half-brother's half-life, or

history's second best – between me
and the indeterminate.
The waves daze me

and all look alike, blending swells and meantooth whitecaps
all one. The house, however, holds
the human, however derivative, diminutive. This

I can tolerate.

But only when

asleep through the wind, the wind
and the whine of gumbo limbo's stretch and
crack, the crawl space beneath the eaves

whirr, roar of the dire wolf's return.

Asleep for the hours needed to hoist mango, strip
avocado branches to bare
bone. Oak and tangle

of palmetto and sweating seagrape, symphony

your ears lay deaf to. Asleep
in the east room, moved away
from the screaming glass, though still

asleep.

The day after betrayed your purpose
betrayed. What lived
clung to exhausted stumps, shaved

raw ridge bone,
all leaves and stalks blown
gone. In

the aftermath, to own your own
terse truth: "No more botany
here. Must go in for

geology." This

I must live with.

# The Lost Nails of John Addison

Here in the clearing Mary sweeps the dirtyard
daily, I imagine. Rises before heat to straw push
the rushes, and fronds aligned, cheek and eyes

south facing. Reading a bone map is like fishing
for snails. They point toward water where water
won't be found. These crust diggers, though,

know ground, panning for shark's teeth
and scallop shells, signs
that life here

was lived. At Addison's landing, flatheads
and brass tacks are fruitful: They amass
and multiply like so many sand grains

left when the shore's long eroded, edged
west. How far did their flat spades poke
to find these nails, and how long lost

was the roof they held highly
in place? I guess Mary needed a cupboard; guests
would land late in November and stay

till spring. Stay to see the seas settle, tradewinds die
and lie calm, the bay steam
with brine and humidity. To plump

pendulant mangoes like warm breasts
they all seemed to relish,
rare and slick, and the avocados they picked

themselves. Chutneys
and marmalade like they never tasted,
swears Mrs. Seabold, and stoneware

to serve it on, gifts from high-placed friends
in Manatee County, hairline cracked, but still good,
still – like me – serviceable.

Like locusts' legs the branches rub their words, your
lifeline, Mary. Dry bone and no kids to ramble
the brackish water, chase owls and flee

sweetly pursuing the one-eyed mockingbirds. Surely
when the tide was out, the fallen branch trampled,
mangrove smell blew ashore. And when

wind pulled from the south, deeper
earth like darkened blood, would cling
for a moment. What wildness

in the dense hammock. Clearing would take
forever. We make
our best guess, sniffing for ridge and rock

where it turns west, circumnavigating
the bowl of sawgrass and herons. Mary
liked to visit, to lunch

with ladies in Cocoanut Grove, to leave
the nails and the hammer sounds, the blood
in the wind, the sounds

of John's dogs and the smells of fish
and sweat, the coontie mess, the roots
revealed at low tide.

She'd prefer her sighs sunk
in the bottom grass, oblivious to rot, lying low, secret
as sweet water.

# Mary Addison Attends a Funeral Not Her Own

Tomorrow's bound to be a better clutch
of hours. There'll be no need
to shadow your mourner's feet

out into the bulrushes, there
with the mud turtles and the red mangrove roots. Then
I can let the time sift through my fingers

wastefully, with sweeter ease, and wash
my resentments like eyesleep from the brood
of sweat-friends and blood kin collected

close towards morning, sending
their words like coiled streamers seaward. Then
I can forget the murk, the silt-grey

milk-dust, the pockets of noon fog that lifted
high off the channel bed dockside, even
the mullets that flew a slapping

salute, once the ashes that were once him
sank some, and rose again.
The glazed May light threw shadows, porous

where the roof pitched unevenly. One
by one, they all left, backing down the drive, down
the road's dead end: Your closure, my

question. Will you mourn me with so long

a lasting sigh?

# Sweat Equity and the Coontie Bonanza

The offer came in a lull time when all craved
improvement – the wild land, the wild boys bound
by the dead end of Bone Key. Four drew
virtual lines in the sand, here

yards from waterbreak, the salt-loving cycads
shouldering through egg-pocked limestone
dust in the dry season, whirlpools of caked starch come
the rains. Through the thick air, four hats – sweat-

feathered like clouds like western salt flats – the heads
overheated, tossed their claims outward, reckoned
from a live oak circled with white stones. In all this –
quite forgettable grows

the coontie green where everything is green. What will be fruit
ripens belowground in pulp-rich pods – arrowroot, good
for baby's colic, the sawgrass heat hunger, surveyors'
stiff white laundry. Only

in muscle memory recalling the harvest – scraping
fibrous tubers, boiling the viscous slurp, bitter
the alkaline bite, but better
than the red poison the leaves sweat, if

not properly vaporized. That's what they mean
by Seminole bread – vengeance lived large. Instead
go barrel the coontie raw when grub gets tight, or
coin's not to be had. The old conch Mabritty

he says this latitude reaps riot or ruin – like chalk-writing
on the seawall, under water's erasure, but the smell
never quits,
no matter what.

# Good-bye to Mar-Y-Cel

Charles Deering had little to no Spanish. Instead,
he spoke a dialect of things. Rubble
cleared from the courtyard meant "Double

my order of bread." Brushed frescoes said
"Guests will be arriving."
In Catalan, we have no words

for hungry hands. Onto the sandstone
beach, cheekbones carved like a coin's surface seen
through the silt, the seaweed, his face

is the merchant assaying dross, scouring
dry acreage. After all the years
trolling inland seas, seeing

the cliffhung palaces cued with arabesque,
keeping seawatch for Old Admiral Case,
to spot wayward currents and North African dust,

now to claim the ruined landfall
calibrating the girth of Moorish ghosts incipient,
sleepwalking, some even healed here.

A risky wreck, this Mar-Y-Cel. How he will remember
the taste of cumin and dark rice, the lure
of El Diablo and Santa Teresa, how they sit

poised, and spar with equal pull. Horns of God's blood
and stormy bulls' testicles, cruel masks,
sweet wine. No sky-eyed sailor set to straddle the prime meridian

could resist this slanting sun, sly-tongued
with a tilda, north now
off Barcelona. My tia recalls

he spoke plain, never fell to bearded language, nothing
to disguise his taste for porcelain, tile inlay,
a silk Portuguese coverlet, sitting,

standing, smelling the wind, saying simply, "In Sitges
where I was happy." When winter orchids
first flowered, they seemed loud that year, even

a little obscene, these
phalaenopsis and their rough vendors, hawking
a young crop. After all

how can it be
these last two, here in the kitchen window
refuse to drop, shrouded

and waxed flat, as if already scrapbook-pressed, and bleached
with dying. They are waiting for this sailing, setting
off with pale petals waving – a ghost's glove

from a starboard window. Packing
is a tune for two, jaunty
and inescapable. We'll share the bench then, and watch

to see him go, to see him watch
to see
the coast recede.

# Marion Wipes Her Hands of It All

Kitty claims the guest bath is a haunted place.
She's seen a brown-skinned hand twirling
the bulb of a mangrove pod. Well,

I hold the holy Shroud of Turin
screened on a fringed terry towel.
My mystery is not knowing

whose face's fragments assemble there
in low light, or when the cloth's rogue droop
converges only through that one

southwest window, or how hotly
someone's wet hands can sculpt a little
of the henna chin, or high cheek. When

was the last time someone used that sink?
Barbara. Still
Barbara. I think

my grandmother must have raised me. She
gave me hot coffee with mostly milk
in the morning, with milk

and mostly sugar, before eight, before sugar became scarce
and taboo, before the breastmilk dried. In the hush
of warm and sweet, where was my mother?

I don't like to see the moon
in the morning, in
the spiderweb hours before

sunrise. Another floating face of someone
gone. I have a friend who thinks
poetry is so easy. The lines

are short, words fortuitous and few.
She can't imagine the chokehold, the
scrum of language that sticks

and dies in the throat, before the ready page turns
a fresh cheek, dry and blank. Objective correlative
of an untutored taste, someone's colorblind

tongue.

# Kitty and the Mock Triumvirate

They'd hole up somewhere upstate.
A woodlot's pace from rough streams that punctuate
rock and run black. No submerged marl-bed
or spring's belly or cave-fed

eddy ever cloyed with salt or crab. Our own
midden creek beyond the boat basin is known
to flow sweet, too, secret and slow by the old
hunting grounds, the mound of skulls, clockwise-rolled,

the owl haunts, the oak. Without mind
like sunflowers, we all turn to freshwater.
We must credit those who flirt

with heat, take on the land's brute air, like salve to unwind
pinched muscles. A pack of them ran hound in later
years. Shock-blurred with Alachua dusk, the damp shirt,

the chigger's chomp, swamp itch,
those loathing and fondling the tolerable temperature mean
the meanness of being poor

and white. One wore the accent, fetched and clutched
by prior arrangement, by appropriation. Then worn heel followed
mean
tongue. And one, sunblind and dead by his will, sure

as spring light. Bolton, he just gave way
to the tin-roofed trailer night. Justice just hoofed a while and held
sway.
And you, Logan, you still just stay.

# Baby Anna Imagines the Future

Where was Mary's apron hanging? Where
in the name of hammock did she find
light and wall for her beaded macrames

her roping vines? Where down in the ever-murking mangrove
could Edith make her mark, and once limned
by the peeling barks, the dangerous saps of tree trunks

how did Marion find water white enough
to filter the pale gauze and suppine chemise
she'd wear to dinner? Sitting

near the old hearth the tapered walls
she could not keep the trace of wild
off her.

# The Bitter Burden of Edith Richmond

I see pride in the belly. It's what counts, what carries them,
what they carry. Like a squatter's bundle slung
from pine rafters still
raw with splinters, snagging rough flax. But

where to hide our misbirths, stuck
stillborn without sight, or where
unwise lungs can scarcely suck
blind thick air?

I thought I bore a ready womb. Not barren, not
barren, not in these resin woods,
these luminous hammocks. Anomalous, the one
who kicks with life only to tithe it

back to the greedy heat. Samuel covets acreage, surveys
direction; I count mangoes, fingers, toes. Baby born
born dead but with residual play
of flailing digits, opposable thumb,

soft skull, brought on
by catastrophic barometer, and lungs still
sea-sponge soft and decidedly
porous, useful to soak

suds off a planked floor, not
the fly-rich air, the larval air
still loud with hum and drone
of dislodged insects. What

feeds this dense earth has left me
nothing, with nothing,
Only eyes, all eyes
gesturing and load-bearing, generative.

Samuel marks the lot bay-facing, sights
the border of our plot, oblivious cairn
of rock plates, hardier marking than the secret tissues
and trailing fibers abandoned in the mangroves --

anonymous the fissures between roots. Amphibious
the thing buried, analogous
the shame.
It all ends

here. So she sits indistinguishable from the dark
hall. Hair still dark
brown still blends with black
air behind her. Black

dog beneath her hand,
hands still, early Sunday. She dreams
cocoons of monarch orange,
like feathers, light webs of sun

like stillborn shrouds. Shift, bend,
sweep sand once
before wedding guests land. Neap tide mud's
no friend to anxious virgins

swaddled in white linen.

# Marion Regrets and Regrets Nothing

How long can I eat
the sun? The dark protein,
the ancient nuclear matter? My clots flare,

and embed your comments, wry
and mean. Oh, there is a shaming wind
spiralling tonight, loose planks

on the front steps, bad fish
on the dinner table, and me
shaking my head like a great wooly bear

pawing flies from honeyed ears. The wax
plumps the hive, its hectic drone
no more the sore distraction. They say

the buzz of invisible locusts in your silent night
precedes deafness. Odd
how the last sound would be

dozing insects in their pre-coital flurry.
Somewhere I read it is their legs
their saw-edged legs rubbing

together like tired joints before sleep. How
could it be that Charles still
hears his night hawks, his mourning

doves and can't hear Kitty's clatter
in the kitchen, egg salad and guava jam
on toast?

The wicker chairs are a nice touch, young
green and sun yellow, destined
in their eventual fade to old mold on bread.

The salt toll here is so severe. Charles amuses himself
sleeping and being read to. He turns
once with each tick, and bastes

neatly as the sentences unfold. Once he is done,
this copper kettle can boil away
with the thunderheads. Meanwhile

I have made all my calls...and
am supposed to be gone by now
by summer, a tedious

mover, like late middle age. Calling me
that back room in the old inn. Bay water, mangroves, sun
invisible, just traces of soil, ribbons of shade

and late day. If asked, tell them Marion's
on holiday, gone
gone to ground with the land crabs, and the succulent

worms the ibises cherish.

# The Brothers Deering and the Reaper Grim

*Apostasioideae*

The Snapper Creek is a likeable stream, Charles decided, like
any place along a briny trail bringing
freshwater gushers into the baking bay deserved

notice, being place name on a map, gift
of future reconnaissance, primitive. The afternoon drifted. Without
much shade, even the thin whites stuck

to his skin like more skin,
like film,
the limp boater slim relief.

*Cypripedioideae*

From the Greek, *orkhis*, meaning
"testicle" because of its flagrant root shape, sings
a term introduced in 1845

by one John Lindley – midway through *School Botany* – a lady slipper
under taxonomies in the order *asparagales,*
containing five subfamilies where stamens and carpels are

fused, seeds are small and one petal of five is always
highly
modified.

*Vanilloideae*

I will come to know this green world, Charles imagined,
like the grass made pliant when soaked
in water, like grass become rope become

baskets to carry grasses like the lemon grass Kitty uses for spiced
meat,
the bitter grass for sickness, the sawgrass that sweeps
the path along the mangrove along

the midden, evolving early and front-ranging in gene sequencing.

*Epidendroideae*

Plant what you like, back-hoe your fake creeks, just keep the green
quiet, no rattling seed pods like unruly woman's tongue, the
ubiquitous
*albezia lebbeck*. Now aboard

the sleek mahogany skiff homogenizing different
tastes, *la vie mode*, *el Diablo*, mother's sweet milk, but could
all jealousies be erased by the pouting colors,

the secret seed-bearing gestures?

*Orchidoideae*

It is a pointed journey pursuing a trail, mobile
through water; yet in odd unannounced lulls comes
phosphorescence of direction, plankton swimming with manatees

in deeper water, boasting
a single fertile species, another evoking
one extinct version, thus ancient

ancient roots. Charles says, I have
no hands, I have
no head. I have

only hands that touch, snip
stalks where blooming
used to be. Twelve months' payload

and the ducks will float and their young
besides and maybe
my stubborn orchids

will bloom.
Reluctant.
Inevitable.

# Marion's Tryst in the Teahouse

Scintillating scotoma
in the late low sun gloom, or
when the barking low sky lisps

snow. Winter in Evanston was no picnic.
Some read cheer
behind the brittle holly, the gasping blue

of high day. This
was to be a refuge, your carefully laid creek
and the house-wide front undressed

to the airflow. Tonight
though, a nasty draft sidles up
between floorboards, up

the gown hem, and the chilling marble sharkbites
my chalk-bone feet. It's never lake-rage alone
would own winter white.

Dark is, wherever dark
congregates. Wherever frond-threads shiver
on branches, wherever

I shiver, remembering
my young bed
my confident fire. Like the sun

when approaching event horizon, secret fault
lines divide all old life from all
that remains, bring the slam

and hiss of shorebreak. You came to biopsy

airplants, core oak trunk rings
on spoil islands, probe the soft boundary

all maps abhor. But imagine color, like
colorblind green-blue
calling forth settlement. I am the victim,

the product of climate's aggression. Most days
I can barely see the season for all the new-sprung pine shacks
among the shaved trees, like painted boxes with small kitchens,

a bedroom off the hall, upcoming sons and daughters measured
with notches in carpenter's pencil on the dining room
threshold. Too shrunk and worn to see how high a child reached

before they came and went. Charles bought
now owns
it all.

I was always only image and emblem of the world
you'd rejected, as you were always
symbol and sign of a world I craved.

It will be best to remain embedded:
emblem, image,
symbol, sign, always

a road not taken, figures
on a vase, a vase
in a poem.

# Mrs. Deering Makes a Withdrawal c. 1928
## *(Imagining Soya e Pomodoro)*

She seemed famous. Not local. Maybe Midwest, in elegant middle age.
She sighed and tapped her stylish bone pump –
little flecks of sandstone and polished rock appeared

beneath the taupe calfskin (slingback, opentoe). Thin sole, so
terrazzo felt cool in the heat of high downtown. Cool here
in the arcade, impressive the fluted columns, brave with the look

of coy money, smug power – simulacrum of tropical gentry, copy
for which no original existed.
Someday, she imagined,
this would be a great place for lunch.

Sniffing for the fictional *bruschetta* she learned to love one summer,
summer tomatoes and mozzarella from Palermo cows – when
oh when would they offer anything in this backwater

besides gristled shrimp and pulled pork, and always always
the obligatory citrus garnish?
Someday, she imagined
a salami of genius would appear, maybe marinated eggplant

and olives and the lovely designer delicacy, sliced thin
as papered tissue, light layered paper in drawers, like translucent
silks, the *prociutto*! Even *Antipasto di Luca*!
She dreamed

a lovely *caprese*, shy and cool, with a thimble of bootleg wine. Someday,
she decided, this cool inside outside would serve something better
than chilled cash. Yes, breathed the thin doyen in beige linen,

it would be a great place for lunch.
She just hoped she'd live long enough to taste it.

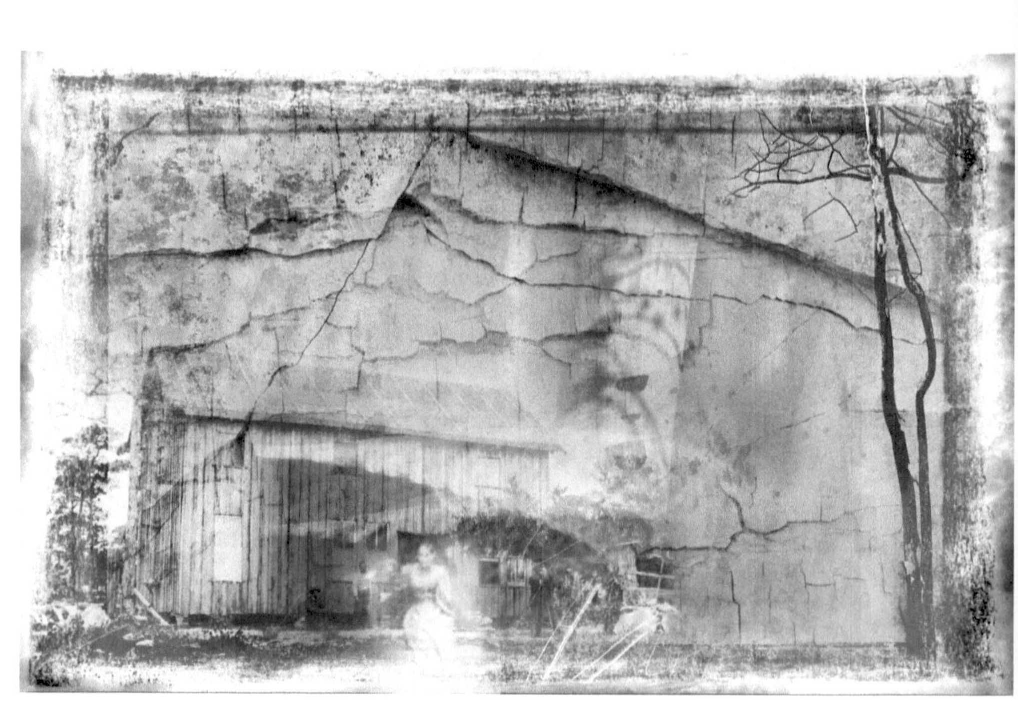

# Barbara Won't Eat

Barbara is a girl who won't
eat who won't eat
with us, with old John Addison, even
young Kitty's pet rabbits. The idea

of opening her mouth, showing bladder-pink
gum, small crooked teeth, or
biting and pulling and chewing
with strangers present. No.

There are some things that must
remain private. When too much body
is exposed, flesh unmasked
from the damask of summer dresses, this

Barbara has never loved. Like love,
certain things thrive in private corners.
An elm tree in Evanston, or
the live oak north of the stone house. Or

afterbirth in the mangroves. Like love
like sex, who can we eat with,
after all? Who won't mind
that we swallow with gusto

with enthusiasm, crush
crunch the meat that glazes our stoneware,
the meat, like love, like secrets,
breathed only in the back bedroom

like the words that say too much. Even
Charles doesn't know how free I am,
how free to speak to you, my virgin page,
my vellum self.

Name me
not by my appetites. To fill you, I won't
be carnivore, or leafy vegan. Proclivities
run along the wire, like the birds that roost

in hot rows.

# Meet Me at Moonrise: Roger Goes West

Phase I: Waxing

Only one road will take you to Hernandez,
and it's a mean given. After
the beef truckers and pork butchers ran west,
and the tourists rushed head
over heels over the mountains, it won't be

seed men and ranchers that greet you tonight.
It won't be me. A flat rash
of white crosses jewel up the wood rot,
the fence posts, tilting toward slack sky
like witching wands staking water, the blunt chill.

The old earth is changing. The light
is toxic.

Who was Hernandez, and why did he pause
here to plant the first corpse? Was he tasting
nascent silver, or remembering a vein
of spiderweb turquoise just shy
of the bedrock?

The clouds are spun milk. The clouds
are vanilla pudding.

Phase II: Waning

I invented a woman who lived under
this moon, and Hernandez was her homeland.
She grew up when the world was black
and white, and the crosses
were salutations. These nights

another town harvests the living,
the wind-rough mothers, the drying
men. Meet me at moonrise, if you'd like, if
you'd like a tour. The sinking grain silos still
host generations of desert bats, and

in the airless dust, tumbleweed will circus roll
with palpable pressure, a secret tide
that flattens oceans, and rolls me here,
thin and boneless, to wait for you. Meet
me at moonrise, when the moon

is most silent, rising without energy. Blown out
Hernandez, a wash of votive candles gone
blank. Meet me after moonrise on the page.
There will be ink enough
in that sky's crude well.

# Like a Bird, Barbara Flies South for the Winter

The plant men say all this once
was ice and before that, water
as far out as the Little Bird Island the island
old Chokoloskee crackers call Chicken Key. Odd. Floating
land mass grounding roots, roosts, immortalizing
poultry. It is impossible
to eat to eat
when food tastes like the dirt
beneath a workman's nails.

# Mr. Deering's Buried Treasure

The boat docks in the new moon's dark, floats
west, fleet and hypnotized along the keyhole channel.
Eusebio brings the low light and eight ready shoulders. Sometimes
a crime is like high tide, flush and miraculous.

The heat is still here. How can any sane self
tolerate damp palms and hair? Here on this south wall
I tend my vineyard. French acreage or
maybe the higher ground of Sonoma

where unasked cool comes masked in artist's oils. Only
the moon at harvest can spread so wide, parabolic
and plumped, juicy like citrus fruit. This fall's first press
is my consolation for exhausted vines, for

this reluctant septuagenarian.

The first sip smooth, first the sweet, not
tart not acidic, just a hint of apple,
oak trace and herbs with no names. Whites and reds
like co-conspirators tiptoeing

to this sturdy vault -- safest hole in the whole place --
where my rock meets your watertable below
ground, stone on stone without mercy
or remorse, gong-deep and oceanbed safe. What

stormgang of law would come so far south
to taste a muscatel? Truth is, what is hidden
is more
than careful vintages.

Wine's first job is to cork the sun, the joy, to graph
hilltrails and grapebuds and child-thin vines
fingerlacing through broken soil, combusting
with nitrate vigor. I like to spy on secret fields

all pokerface and curious, like shy scrubbed boys
late for the prom, flirting and dodging a clammy
and covetous hand. Some spring, I'd like to wallow
in mustard hedge, the callow yellow

that shoulders the vine-rows, the color waste, to lure
the humming bees and lull a dozen types
of dozing sweets. So how is it done,
this water to wine? Just rest

and dream of grapes, skin shallow and swollen, soon
to surrender their lucre, a long labor that tonight
gives me grace, gives me harvest, the push
and rush of harvest moon.

# The Dirge of Marion Deering

I am the world's secret monster – a woman
in the change. Who can breathe breathe in

this heat. What is that noise, locusts or crickets? I know –
it's late summer and the locusts are starting

to rub their legs – the anticipation
of anonymous death and dry husk rictus.

We all sit in sweat and sweat. And
there are many like us,

silent mammals
shivering with sour glands,

dry teeth. What used to be arresting
and deliciously epithelial

now creeps in dizzying zigzags, lacy lines
across an exhausted décolletage. No joy

no savor
no milk. This is the world of women when

estrus ends. We eke comfort
from the air. Once we've survived

all the rest, the fatigue of courtship,
the wife's settling, hormonal kaleidoscope

and child raising, child leaving, once
we are left in large houses with quiet cats

we can breathe and smell the afternoon. Who is grilling,
whose grass has been cut, who has recently

left her house, locked the front door, taking
her perfumed arms out

into the early evening.

# Edith and the Black Dog

I don't recognize my hands
and what to make of this old scar, hardly
decipherable, like wolf tracks through fog. The folds
of years and liver pigment party
to mask it. Just fossilized

teeth traces of a dog startled
up, protecting sleep's muffle, or
dreams of a secret kill, or
an offspring's hungry mucus eyes, still
shut in birth's revery. She is long swept,

all ashes and atmosphere, except
for the vacancy warmed by her absence.
Take these scars. Three unlikely lines
perpendicular to a calcifying grip. With scrutiny,
they fade. I remember the feel of her, recognize her

fur under my human hand.

# Old Anna Sweeps the Midden

Where does the yellow go when the light thins
with time? It is a change of color, a sinking haze that watches
heat and bile go, harvesting the aftertraces, silo stacking
yards of cornsilk no longer viable, without regret. Faint
residue, like an echoing scent serves to remind to
remember. I see ghosts of children sailing across asphalt,
chasing a runaway black dog, maybe a far hit softball,
a rogue kite, laughing. They never fear permanent
lift beyond their grasp, however mildewed their fingers,
or sweet with candy traces, or damp
with one last lick. Yellow yellow light
in that southwest exposure, now just because
it is late February because
the snow's found ways to melt where it fell because
we are the lightkeepers, custodians of the air's gold
until the time comes and the baby coots come
and the new brood of all sleepwalkers come
and rub their lazy eyes.

# Eusebio Strikes the Lost Chord

Summer was finished early
yesterday when the west coast team
took home the trophy. Fans and players

danced and swung themselves dizzy, sucking
large gulps of victory from the laughing air. Like
swallowing sweet cream on fire, tongue so numb

the victory unpronounceable. He always loved
baseball, though he didn't know he always loved
summer. November was never this cold never

not even in East Santa Rosa when he was small and
the earth spun sideways through ruined smears
of winter when it was time to draw rows

in fields and pray for plump beans, and tomatoes
flamboyantly red. But the red mercury careened
as he breathed red hot before the glass tube mounted

outside Kitty's pantry. You'd think
the heat of stones and tended hearth would warm
the settlement, rush the first red light at dusk

when the porch chairs and the lately laid
concrete pavers grew indistinguishable
and spiderwebs wasted with unnamed things

and their underground stirrings. He'd never planted
a body gone to seed, but the air near his shoe soles leeched
formaldehyde busy at work and ready

to run away with itself.

# Aggie Young and the Fogs of Spring

The linen came from Egypt, or
maybe Syracuse, New York. The groom
was conspicuously absent.

In the moment's apostrophe, the need
to sit frozen as the big-boned Land camera chased
fractals onto one silver-treated

8x10 plate. Buddy! He jerked, clowned,
blurred. You hadn't arrived. We went on
without you, Wilfred. Even

after a three-fingered anodyne, the wolfbite
still ached and the bride convalesced
within the vertigo of the third person. Up

in the north parlor, the fan turns
slowly. Turns with the wet gusts, unseasonable
damp creaked the floorboards, whose steps?

Mrs. Edith rode uptown
earlier, wants her beeswax for the banisters, the trim
molding, the public floors, the air fogged

with tangerine and frankincense. Where
was Wilfred? Where the road, where
the membrane separating woman from wife, where

did night's warm muffle end and sharp
light start? Is this how marriage is? My white dress
and your furtive tie, starched collar,

fugitive intentions?

# Barbara Gets the Ugly Boat

Could have been a bridal morning when workmen crossed
the channel, beam bursting on the dowdy Barbee
just back from the mouth of Crocodile Hole dragging
flowers, flowers, flowers,

wild weedy flowers and pungent roots --
Monday's mudwash draping the teak's splintering rail.
Parakeet ferns, bromeliads and orchids
trailing their five vestigial fingers

through the shallows, reading
the keyhole's dredged hips
like floral braille. Even the blind

could see two sisters separating, blonde
and not blonde, not
when SOMEONE

vagabonds to Paris, cauterized at 28 and
debuting her thick
calves for an eligible
McCormick, and SOMEONE

remains to throat-swallow their bile,
their nascent wail. So her ship sailed. All hers
the mung-oiled posh, the mahogany in estrus, the bleached pursars

balancing mimosas, lap-straked hull,
deep keel. Parallel that tender wave and
far from the fabled Kingman mines and

their catacombs for sleeping beauties, Charon just polls
and polls. Unknowing, they each gave
their mother a sky stone, something

dirty blue for a wilted bride long past
perfect tense, mistress of tired botany and prosthetics. So the
prodigal
sailed. So groomed, the

parents mourned, imagined
what would never escape
that phosphorescent wake. Do

you see these ragtag swatches? Thus assembled?
thus unraveling? They confess a coat of mixed intentions –
a parent's gift to the lesser child. But when you ask

they always say
they loved you both
the same. Deaf, the same

to Barbara making music
inside her body, her humming
body's lullaby to her own

inward
turning
ears. Alive, her boat ferrying

chromosomes and
mulch, mulch
and chromosomes.

# Handover at Wildwood – A Song for Surveyors

"Where are you?"
The map would begin here
at Buddy's Bar-B-Que, Home of the Smoking Pig. Or maybe
inside the thumb-pinched crust of pecan pie
and the rolled dough, or
the day they rolled the dough somewhere

in a small bungalow south of Ocala, the day
that needed more shade,
the cloudy bright day, languishing
with disinterest and sore neglect. Not
a place for the silk-and-linen crowd, the cash cows,
unsuitable for those divining water, seabirds, water.

Buddy's has closed. Blank
the side door to the service kitchen, the loading dock, awaiting
the next joint venture to stack rough-hammered crates,
ship produce, and trade
leftover pecan pie congealed on a dixie plate
wrapped in foil, hand-smoothed foil

loosened by the play of inattentive hands
opening and closing the folds too often.
"I don't know," Samuel answered.
Somewhere in the grumbling underbrush bounding
the perimeter, Mack trucks ascend the on-ramp back
into the hazy fall afternoon, cooling.

Autumn's firepit is proof how even wet wood can spark,
breed warmth for unseen small creatures in the bush, safe
from large mammals with hunger pangs, marking
domain. Still, male scent scores the crossroads
intersecting surveyor's tool and latent appetite
for tillable acreage.

Two oak leaves in the thin sun.
Known earth ends here, can't
harvest the salt, the stone-pocked south. Or
laurel leaves splattered by unseasonable rain. Cloudy bright. This
was the forecast they'd recall in the slanted sunshadow that flamed
dull leaves to stencils, trapped in gutters of mixed mud,

oil spill-off. Webster's cattle prices are off
this year. Something about lean feed and a dry
summer gone flat. "Except
in the wild woods…" It was just a slice of pie, seemed
a fair trade, but somehow sold
short. The pecan's lost its snap,

and the stale crust offends his taste buds salt
to bitter, crumb trails dogging telegraph lines
strung ever southward. Homage to one Isaac Barwick,
his fledgling company first on the map – indicia of surveyors – but no
answer why the lynx-tailed cotton grown by white men in Georgia sold
for a better price in Silver Springs.

# Outcroppings

Part One: The Great Bone Oak Laments

Henry Perrine returned to prove a point
to steal a skull, as if
so crude a vengeance could

delete the dreams of crouching fetal
and hidden in the ground, a hidden
grave. Flies and wind conspired

drove him blind to all things green,
especially during winter in a place
that balances bones

and horticultural riddles.

All the green
points to
all the black

of the vacant midden, so like
my own midden my own midlife
compost heap. Amid shells,

quail wings, buckets
full of crawfish exoskeletons, forms
a new shoreline, height, a hill

where there was none. And
yards away
Venetian lace and English net marry

the sharp smell of decaying shrimp,
egret bones sucked clean,
white as the noon light.

## Part Two: A Calculus of Bones

The pull and strict gravities fortify
when I travel due east. An invisible sheerline, like
latitude, with railroad tracks struck perpendicular, then

the surveyor's mark, a cottage of carpenter's joints
and Dade County pine breaking like waves
into the dozing bay. Then

there were fish -- grouper, snapper -- full bore
with the trade winds, the shore,
the calling.

## Part Three: Oolite and Orchids

To the naked eye, they
couldn't be farther apart. A part
of rockbed's subcutaneous web where sweet

water flows, oolite egglike, and ovum chambers
for water seed and snail bones. Now
the fairy orchid, that's another

story. Nothing is more elaborate
or provocative. Posing inside out
and in color.

## Part Four: Song of the Cottonmouth

What if the owl's face were transparent? If
we could see behind the feathered bonegrid, behind
the lidless, blinkless eyes? There's some

wisdom as she roosts, nests
new great-horned guardians like herself, hidden
in the hollow center, history's

great sieve.

Roots can trip you. Stay near the ridge. Roost
where the eggs nest. The oolite eggstone
facilitating the water.

They all say this.

Poisonwood, disguised by moss
and the lichen patchwork marking
the trunk, camouflaging

the toxic sap within. A syrup to blister
the skin and worse.
Allergic reaction,

pathogenic as death. This, and

I worry about the seed of old parents, old
tired plants. Is it hardy enough
serious enough to undergo

mitosis?

## Part Five: When Bones Speak

The living bonescape, a pinwheel
cell, core-facing
like starfruit circling

a moment of ridge and oak pre-natal
pre-Columbian, when
the rock was young

spongy and
widely impressionable.
Leaves of hair, fine

hair of arms on
skin, crooks of elbows and knee joints
now old, arthritic from water damage

oolitic drainage and wind
crooning the oak
and the fifteen chiefs.

Part Six: Cayo Hueso and North

You could smell them before
they appeared. A hole
wide enough to cradle the bones

of dire wolf, peccary,
wooly mammoth, those that hobbled
themselves to sate appetites, those

that prayed for calm
after storms. It was a good smell:
earth, and roots, something green, but

hovering, the mean tang of poisonwood,
black
as tar, and vicious

like the aery delicacy of poison ivy,
my childhood dreams of poison oak
and the lethal kiss

we called poison sumac.
Merely footfalls
from road-dust and the surge

of catalytic converters, the mottled dress
of fatal touch, the oily saliva
of trees' mouths graphed a fence, a fencepost

to keep them
from us, us
from them. The cave

was dimly lit, roots
led the way to the sink floor, acid
eroding limestone, sculpting secret quarries.

I feared the smell, imagining
that's what bones drying
in the earth must be like, like

my mother's bones
still trailing bits of exposed marrow or
tissue. But no. It was as if

from a distance. Not grave,
but ground, all incipience and plenitude.
This, but

the peninsula was for me the end,
the zero mile of a long, tired continent. Yet
maybe land's end where limestone

breaches bay or the straits
is, in fact, generative – the elbow crook where
coastal rock ridge turns in,

the curved arm cradling
the still soft skull, the mother
lode, the bones forming,

still to be formed.

# The Deconstruction of Charles Deering: Birdsong

*cau-cau-cau-cau-CAU-cau*
The creek isn't aligning
to plan, the wall
sports chinks and fissures. This

beyond the dirt taste
of well water. Yet
Kitty carries inside her apron

twelve cupcakes
with pink icing, a thin waxed sheet
screening the unpredictable

kiss of strawberry. Least Bittern
approaches. Charles deaf to salt-caw
craves the marsh rush.

*ahk, ahk, AHK-AHK, ahk*
A bone
becomes a rock
becomes a tree. These

subtle algorithms multiplying
shorebirds, nesting pairs intent,
preening the glossy black, red

mouth inside. Fish-crows undetected
and repurposing split carrion
among the drowsing weeds. He

smells lowtide. The bragging rights
of mating pairs. Can
cut throats sing?

*tsh-whew-HEO-whew*
Chuck-Will's-Widow has it. The eyeshine.
Something about infrared's twang and planet's
invisible curvature, glow

that refracts in the tired evening of late light.
Motionless through the water's slop against seawall –
certain of the oncoming imperative

the tireless call. He
is wheeled to catch the dusk, sniff
bay mud's brine at midsummer cross-quarter.

He will write "Excuse pencil, bad writing. All
is hard enough." The high-coffered ceiling
in the grand space facing east held

Brahms in those scalloped edges, echoed
against deep marble exiled
from Siena hillsides. He

always preferred white linen trousers,
a new straw boater each season. The wind
would lift the brim, set sail its frivolous

band. He liked to pluck fresh grass shoots
in summer, the wide ones worked best, hold
twin thumbs close on the cool seam, place

his lips close by and blow. A
boy's wet whistle. Called
the spirit. Called

the gods. Called
the birds.

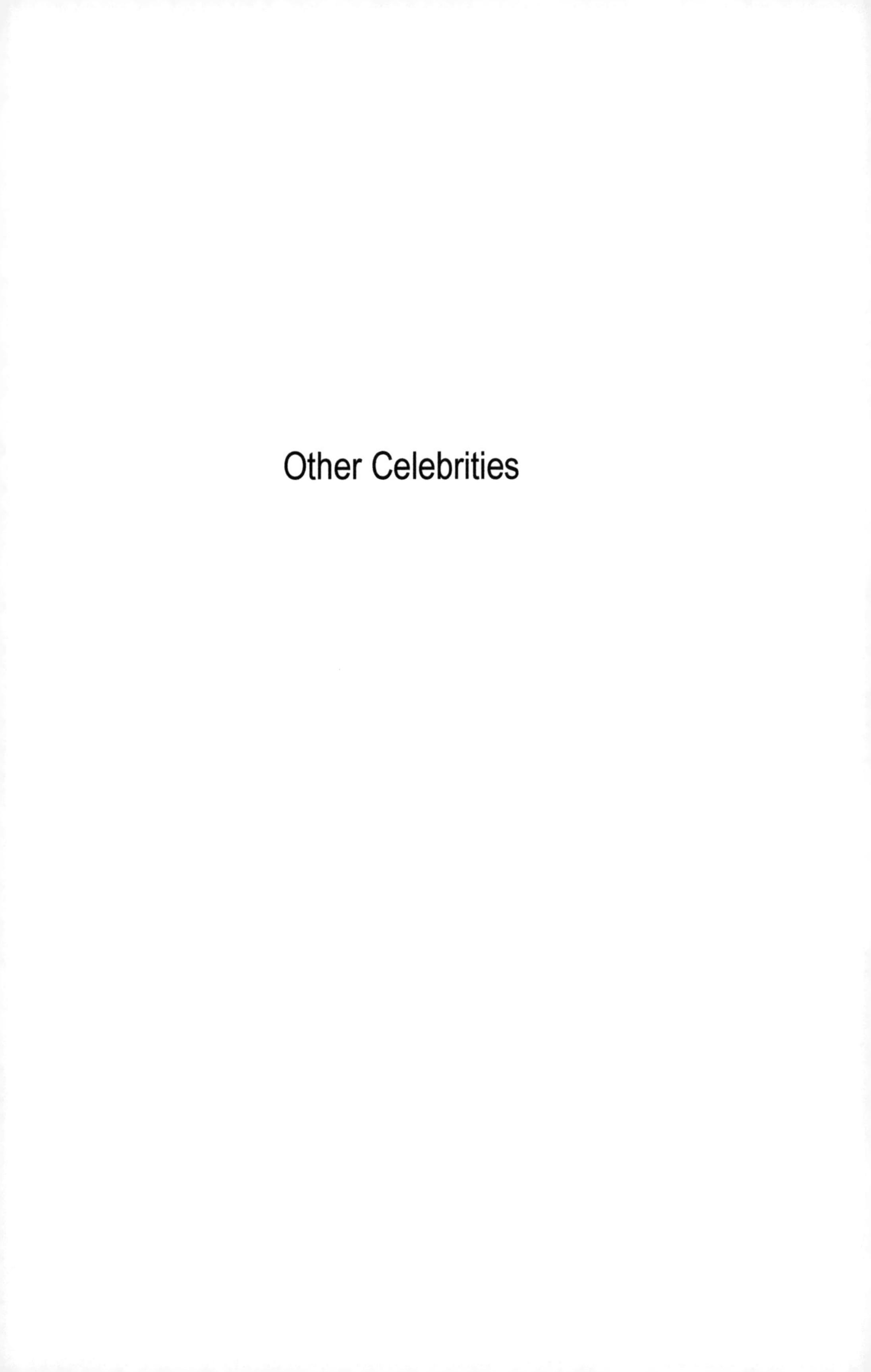

# Other Celebrities

# Ismene Upstaged

Ismene of the bottlebrush tree, how long
can an eyebrow grow untweezed? What if
it's left to curl and punk-jut

garden-random, scalp,

eardrum, cornea, liberated
as milkweed? How will you ever learn
the proper shape or coax of comb

to settle these tantrum hairs? At eleven,
this is gnosis: the wafers of initiates,
bitter gift to put tongue to, to find

browbone's right trace, the latent surprise and sweep. Until

that first tug is made, maidenhair is sand, silk,
the sibillant outbreath splitting water
from dryland. This brown diadem,

lighter than oak leaves, what

final curve or line – snarl or question --
waits disguised? Still grumpy and attractively bedridden,
a roaring god beneath marble vein, still

covert.

I make a hobby of scanning brows for scars
like yours: graphite hashmarks, swift strokes presage
the capitulation to come, soon enough. For now,

incorporeal, fixed by a mother's shadow some summer
after school lets out. Neither famous
nor tragic, you'll blend in

well.

# Vivienne Haigh-Wood Prefers Milk to Eggs

But I am not a good mother, she said. I let
the milk go bad. Beyond
the sale date, by more than a week, and still

not replaced in the hour with something still remembering
the udder's roll and squeeze. What kind of mother
lets the milk go sour? Lets

the white cow-juice curdle, lets
the mooing calves feed, fend
for themselves? How can she let

the kids go hungry, their hooting mouths cawing
for more? Down on the farm,
they understand this. Here

uptown, they just wonder. Me,

I just like the market on sale day.

You ask about the dream.

In the dream it was all earth, and earth smell
rubbed on crisp cotton,
smudged on skin. It was hard to tell

whether you, you the sovereign
of matter, mother, were battling
the slugs, pinching their insistent presence

out with your cool, capable fingers, or
parting the furrows, the channels
of worm-road to carry

me down. Either way, it is clear I missed you
as much as you
missed me.

All mothers must
return to the dust. Trust
that the rightness of things

will exonerate short life, brief
stay, long
sorrow. Our idle hands

hopefully more than worn welcomes,
home base for latch-key children who bikeride
through the afternoon, when

there's
more light
from the south –lighter the east sun's

burn, unclenched the bun-knot unclipped
and brooding west, crow's nest lookout
loosening. Sun

moving south, south, south
beckons. I, for one,
am not sorry to see it go. Just

one stray hair of light
on the pillow
where her head nested in sweet

sleep sweet dreams. Now
that is a light I could learn
to love.

You laid me
like an egg. That's
the cracking noise I hear
inside my head. Me
trying to get out
after this fearfully
long incubation.

# A Second Mirror for Sylvia

Mirrors mean nothing. Why then dream
seven years' bad luck when
they break? Step back

and see the design deficiency in that glass
backed with corrugated, and silver backed, now
long since like the long oblong

sides – deconstructed. There, you'd check

your look. Wet curls, kohl-lined
eyes like almond slices, sometimes brown
or grass green, the finishing last look lingering, looking

at me, even after you'd leave for work. Your portrait
now long since, like the sides,
deconstructed. So with you

it all went, when you left.

Bags and boxed clothes, your name, sewn
at the neck, visible to my eyes
only. The mirror I kept long

where you left it. Would readjust
the broken frame, passing time, from time
to time. But that room emptied, filled

with wakes, unseen scent cells, a sole lost slipper.

So the mirror was trashed, though no one cares, or
dares to fold it, jam its cardboard spine, peeled
and weathered with ruin, rain, to risk

breaking the looking

glass spell. No. But
from time to time, I'll side step

to peek into the surface, now

facing only the rough grout ground, gone
of grass, just loops of pool plumbing nearby
left over rock, to risk a quick

look, and maybe see some residue

of your face, still there waiting
to recognize me
before trash day.

You taught me to trust my mirrors.
Not to doubt the slowly
receding line, the vertiginous parallax, left

is right, but

to trust that small objects
will seem larger and
closer, yes

but trust that the wheels will move

in reverse, the driveway will end
all the same, where
paved blacktop and pocked asphalt meet strands

and strands (your hair left in the winds of brushes left) and

strands of braided St. Augustine runners, bred
to resist drought, mites,
and dissolution.

# Mary Brickell's Tomb

Brenda and Joe's Bismarck palm finally
took root. This was after two previous attempts
to anchor, sink deep and puncture

the high-strung limestone –

screeching all the way with the pickaxe
and the ferocious grit of shoulder, the gait, yet
nothing – until

finally one seemed satisfied here, a hump
of a hill on the bank, as if to say, sigh,
I'll witness your winters,

your expectant arrivals,
forsaken departures – the coming and going
of great blue herons,

determined egrets. After all,
winter won't last. The grey-
green fan dance, once dug in and coral wed

leaves nothing to chance, or choice.

Where will we sleep tonight, Mary?
Tonight you sleep beneath my roof, dancing
on my soft-sodded grave, deliberate

in my dreams. I watch
your eyelids flutter,
hieroglyphics of midnight sun. "This

is my winter

time. My version of cozying in,

daylight and hothouse sun simmering
the not negligible pleasure of squinting

in the afternoon, with the blinds closed, light still
loose, red scarf on the western front. It never feels
like December when days lurch

quick toward the last calendar page. By this time
I'm bored with the year, and ready
for another go." This

is my winter, skimming
out of sunreach and off the map. Always
in late afternoon, always with slim

threads of light left, no regret
or pale hankering after fatter flowerings,
content, in fact, jubilant

in this modest poverty, the dire stores, grim
Thanksgiving, meager
ecstasies. Stolen

this time, the mute caches
my hoard for sunrise,
sea-rise, when what remains melts

glaciers.

The afternoon at Mary Brickell's tomb was heavy,
pressed with cloud and winter cover, not dark yet,
not so late then, but breathless

and still like Sunday. This

was no graveyard, just a bland lawn of settlers' acres
undeveloped, nothing commercial zoned
or inhabited at all, and we

had the run of the place.

Mary, where will we sleep finally? First crib,
last cradle and crib
bumper, edged in eyelet,

pillowing the brunt
of bruised, still soft skull, burrowing
finding the deepest hollow, secret saliva

trail, aphrodisiac, this longing for

my weaned young.

I still have this dream of short days, or maybe
just leaking memory, a spillover
from rooms, voice crowded and clothes

on the floor. Several voices at once, the tag and push
of punchlines, stove burnt
with a twist, tongue's surprise –

the dazzle of joy, white chocolate
on strawberries, winter's fruit, sweet
and extravagant. If early dark,

short life has a flavor, this

would be it.

# Stanley Kunitz's Gardens
*--for Carlo*

They are Masai, you said, and it was their spring. Wake
and the high currents of east wind send
hawks to mammal, all dog-eat-

dog, when midair scrapple

snaps the skystring, and to earth
the feathers fall, twisted twig bones. Or
perhaps it was the old one, or

the smallest's turn. Sky now seems dayround empty, only

so many field mice show their necks,
their vulnerable succulence. The dung air
says, Plant soon, count cattle, play

quickly. This leathery handful
fills her arms, her chaste noon
as the black crakes fly ecstatic --

the air balletic, slim-hipped and
long of thigh, slender foot,
wide wings. Alive as long as

we let them. Could they

dream of days when the sun was wider
than the savannah, the alluvial fields
where dust and earth conjecture

lucidity, dreams higher than thought, than singular

insight? The lilytrotters advance
along with the fish eagles,

the haughty ospreys. This one

left behind becomes a baby doll to carry, to finger-comb

and smooth the coy-rooted scalp. Wingspan
wide arms held out for her, bug-curved
mouth crying for sustenance. Bright-eyed, but

set to sleep, and cornered

within the crook of arms bent, still flat-chest nestled. Yet
the bean eyes won't close – Wadi gnats circle
the irises until her hands

can do their work. Which sister will walk

that dead bird to the cradle, swipe
flies from its lashes? Strange how this plump doll
begins to moult, feathers

loosen, leaving a falling trail like fallen leaves
behind the Provincetown house away, away, to mulch
your autumn garden. But here, you say,

it's spring, until all
will ground in ground
old bird, old man, beak to beak, to old earth.

Is it worse to lose the one life destined to end short, or
the one with the long ago lost start? And you
could hold her only for so long. Not really

time enough for the feel of the bones to grow
familiar, with ease to count the intervals
between padded feet and shoulder's hollow. What

would her spring have been like, her pupils
to contract and filter deepening light,
higher sun. And the heat, what of the heat

until summer's end? But
even that was too much for cheap time, blunt February
to grant. It's not hard staying here, wrestling

with these dead birds, old
bird-beaked dead man. Better this than small cats
that go down, young and easy. And my old arms too old

and can't comfort too young
you, your arms too
empty.

# Little Jeannie Turns 30

It was the summer when Little Jeannie
packed the house. She was the soundtrack
for grudging detente, two horn-locked parties
deciding to bury their arms –
plant ambitious rows of field corn

cloned to reprise the earth songs of hunters
and gatherers, domesticated animals. She was
a hawk's sister, milk cow's mother. She was
you, Kali-fondled avatar of the first born,
the womb breaker. Enough. For 30 years,

I've wondered what size shoe
your Cinderella sole would eventually fit, whether
you'd like surfing
or sand dollars, oil or vinegar. Whether
your teeth would crave salt or sweet.

Little Jeannie, your fable curtailed, mattering not
nearly long enough to grow eyes, no tongue
to taste, ears to hear your number one single
top the charts, and play out
its antiphonic revery.

# The Death of Jane Kenyon

She makes a handsome run of it, a gloved handful's
grab with one hand clapping, some summer's firefly
half-life incandescence jar-trapped, subtle

seedless grapes served as dessert – pale and white green

from California. Sweet bites before evening

falls.

I know if I just held her head, maybe touched
the fine bones beneath the scalp's robin-feathering, or
smoothed the last swirls of rabbit grey, last

light in the autumn sky or
stood champion beside the basin as she upswilled
poison, expelled cells that sank

life's buoyancy, leadened down
her words, compromised her walk, matted
her cancer

hair.

Entering the honeycomb of language, delectable byways but
I can't find you among these prisonyard turns,
ruins, sanctioned release beyond the barbed wire, Jane. Remaining

a tear of paisley hem, tortoiseshell
toggle button, graphite shavings and random false starts under
erasure. They will study you

under imagery. Find you in an extra copy left
on the desk after class's

dismissal.

Where does this leave me? I plucked
words in season from bramble bushes, the brackish
silk weeds, sea oats by bay's salt side

suckled on orange blossoms and rind, even
the bitter sap stirred my taste, one day
in hiding, taken out of context, light from

light.

# Hildegard & the Rising Fifth

[Hildegard of Bingen was a 12th Century writer and composer of unforgettable choral music which brought church plainchant to a highly individual art. Her use of the ascending fifth, rather uncommon in earlier liturgical pieces, became her signature, her thumbprint.]

It's a turn of phrase
just a lilt of notes that soars
through this old stone, the choir's eagle's nest,
the spectrum shift of leaded glass that moves you. Memories

hatch like ducklings. It wasn't always this way. Memories

of morning hours outside Mainz, warm
with milk and shadowing belled cows,
ox-eyed daisies – symphonies of the painted season.

Disembodied leaves of birch and elm in autumn, the scoop and fly
when heat returns to hills' climb. Sweat, your muddied hems,
and the smell of slow beasts and umber soil rich in iron. The iron

convent gates wax-sealed the silence, the stiffening, a stifling death

in life until the voices,

their gathered voices break
fast like flutes or
soft-strung lyres
rising as wood smoke through braided thatch,
song-shaped,
the iconic air of assembled days.

It's a croon of hum
just an arch of breath that ascends with the sparrows, invisible
spirit-space, without predefined length or width, where pointed spires
press heaven. You remember

the wind in winter, whistling, with cold feet,
the inside drafts, the drifts
like fallen clouds. They say

it was visions, a dream of singing angels in tiaras
with sparkling rings, one for each finger
echoing the shine of virgins, their hair unbound.

But no. You remember

human women with baskets of dried fruit, chewing cherry bark, men
with hatchets, hewing pine, massaging pitch and tar,
their baritones chest-deep in desiduous leaves,

and always the singing hands at work, mostly your mother's
smoothing stubborn hair, the voices weaving ribbons and yarn-spun
bows,
the surprise when the shyest girl hits

the highest note

with dazzling splendor.

# Carolyn Heilbrun and Meg's Baby

Carolyn, don't believe me
but I think I've mastered the drag
the droop of sagged flesh, the pull of grave

and gravity. So after

some allotted years of posed faces from wall-hung
to wallet-sized, chirping fixed at sixteen
and hiding ten painted toes beneath

gag socks. But before

my old smell, familiar as a dresser drawer
will sweat from jaded walls
and sour skin long down

in the heels, just adjusting photos dreaming dust
with other chef-tossed relics
under glass.

After, before and here so horn-straddled uploads
the desire to devolve into that six-week sonogram, be the smiling
embryo with the beehive hair, streaming

like lithe fingers through silk,
the sac of fluid that sets the swimmer born
free. Or be the mother high-geared to grunt and carry. Carolyn,

apparently seventy is less free than this.

Your printed name bellows, gong bellweather
for the decades, the quick talk
the multisyllabic quickened bits, book by book

we queued to buy, to bed with

our fearless foremother in sensible shoes
pimping swallowed time, leading.

Somewhere I read that you used to lunch ladylike
every odd Tuesday, holding court
at Tavern-on-the-Green – Waldorf salad chilled

with a side, smug, chewing contented
cuds. When did the iceberg limp flat,
bitter, the dilated crowd between the Met

and Macy's become braying, upstarting a sense
long since gone to seed, the sleeping hayloft
of the upper 80s, as all cinderdust

from vented sidewalks and snow turned –
when you turned in the key –
lung grey. Maybe someone should tell

Meg's baby. Maybe someone should

tell Meg.

# Mary Kinzie's Last Word

*Threshold* is a first word to conjure
the composting cosmos. And she spins it
whirling dervish style, a wheelie

on Christian Hosoi's old splintered board
upended somewhere near Santa Monica pier
where the old bronzed boys

with oiled chests touched the half moon
the Pacific Rim, breaching
their own event horizons.

DIEBOLD
Safe&Lock

# You Remind Me of Days --
## *for Bob & Susan Arnold*

At first I thought you were old, old forest bears,
grizzled old because Vermont is old, as old as the skyworn
mountains, soft felted flannel. Years

ago, we spent a long weekend, three days near
the White River, the White River
Junction was the map's place, near

where the house was. It belonged to someone
someone else knew. Still unfinished, though,
raw shellac raking everyone's

eyes. Lots of sawn wood from the white birch rising there
on the property, up the hill slope, slant surveyed, down
to the River. Even there –

where the house was new – it all seemed old, old
trees, old sky, and because it was young
July, the sun was warm on my back, the soil still cold.

# Harvest Done (And Gone)
## *For Andy*

This high drama the high plains knows. They
are bringing the harvest all golden in golden
all summer long

nitrates drove cell walls green
followed glucose followed
green sunk earthward

skybound birthed glutens gone golden, now they
are bringing the harvest
in. In

this middle world, this
hypothetical season, Indian Summer's breach, until
leaves fall in earnest, and they

bring the harvest in. Not
the high green push of kernels
a-sugaring, or grain-crowded

with plumped chaff, droving
combines scything the crop, cracking the seeds,
bringing bringing the harvest

in. I've come this late to hear the husks,
the dry rustle, the brown twilight,
the breathing ground, not

wheat not corn-yellow and systematically cellular, just

old green gone after green
is done, after

the harvest
is done. They already know autumn's
ciphering dust, leaves leap-leaving

the faith-leap that ground will succor. They
hear geese roused before the weather
and their marshy landing south

on low-lying coasts. They know
the harvest is ready ready to bring
the harvest

in. Before the incipient rain
sour-seeds the stalks
when they bring in the sunchairs

the beach towels, the coal-greased grills, last
residues of August meat. They bring in
long summer's long work, their harvest

done.

*Autumn 2011*
*Champaign, Illinois*

C.M. Clark's poetry has appeared in a variety of publications, including *Painted Bride Quarterly*, *Gulf Stream* magazine, and the inaugural Florida Center for the Literary Arts anthology *Write Here*. She participated in a program featuring South Florida poets at the Miami Book Fair International and has served as Poet-in-Residence at the Deering Estate in Miami. Clark's previous work was published in *The Blue Hour* (Three Stars Press, 2007), and in the artbook *Pillow Talk*. Pieces included in this current collection have been displayed as illustrated broadsides at the SoBay Arts Festival in Miami, and in a collaborative presentation at the 8th Annual Boneyard Arts Festival in Champaign, Illinois. She has been a regular contributor to the multicultural online journal, *Asili,* and her work was featured in Geoffrey *Philp's Blog Spot*, a review of Florida and Caribbean writers. Clark lives with her husband in Miami, Florida.

www.ingramcontent.com/pod-product-compliance
Ingram Content Group UK Ltd.
Pitfield, Milton Keynes, MK11 3LW, UK
UKHW040558210726
13854UKWH00008B/1481

9 781105 618338